Railway Memories

WARRINGTON

Compiled by Stephen Chapman
With pictures by Arthur Chester

BELLCODE BOOKS
10 RIDGE BANK TODMORDEN
WEST YORKSHIRE OL14 7BA

Copyright © 1996 Bellcode Books

ISBN 1 871233 08 9

Edited by Stephen Chapman

Printed by The Amadeus Press Ltd, Huddersfield.

ABOVE: Bank Quay station in steam. A Stanier Black Five 4-6-0 takes water while awaiting departure for the north. Warrington No.2 signal box stands aloof on the right and Liverpool Road bridge straight ahead. *(P. Norton collection)*

FRONT COVER: The high spot of any day at Bank Quay. The all red Glasgow to Euston Caledonian rolls in hauled by Stanier class 8P Coronation Pacific No. 46246 *City of Manchester* during March, **1961.** *(B. Magilton / Colour-Rail)*

BACK COVER TOP: Chester-based BR Standard class 5 4-6-0 No. 73025 was well turned out in the mid-1960s for duty on southbound covered hopper wagons, pictured on the West Coast main line near Walton New Junction.

BACK COVER BOTTOM: Already just a memory are the loco-hauled expresses which ran on the Cheshire Lines in the 1980s. Brush Type 2(class 31) No. 31435 arrives at Warrington Central with the 13.22 Sheffield to Liverpool on 28th April, 1988. *(Stephen Chapman)*

INTRODUCTION

Warrington marks a departure from the usual Railway Memories stamping ground east of the Pennines and we welcome readers in the North West who may be setting eyes on one of these books for the first time.

Details of other current Railway Memories books are given inside the back cover.

Although never mentioned in the same breath as Crewe, Doncaster or Swindon, Warrington has remained an important hub in the national rail network for 160 years, especially where freight is concerned. Its geographical position and wide range of manufacturing industries have seen to that.

The presence of the London-Glasgow main line and a multitude of large industrial plants meant that everything from glamorous express trains to little shunting engines could be seen inside just a few square miles.

The sudden availability of unique material by former railwayman Arthur Chester made a book covering the five miles from Acton Grange to Winwick a prospect too good to resist.

Arthur Chester was a well-known character around the railway in the 1960s and 70s,

when he was a shunter at Walton Old Junction and did some work as a guard. He took his camera to work and never missed an opportunity for a good picture.

Railway Memories No. 9 celebrates his foresight in using his camera liberally and expertly. Unless otherwise stated, all pictures in this book were taken by Arthur Chester, supplied by courtesy of Tony Cook.

By the time this picture was taken, a steam-hauled express was clearly a major attraction at Bank Quay station. BR Standard Britannia Pacific No. 70035 *Rudyard Kipling* awaiting departure for Crewe was the source of all the excitement on 2nd September, 1967. (*Peter Rose*)

SETTING THE SCENE

Warrington may not have the status or glamour of Crewe, Preston or Carlisle, but as any railwayman and enthusiast knows, it is a railway centre of vital importance.

The marshalling yards stretching for nearly a mile to the south of Bank Quay station produce a scene of railway activity rarely seen in Britain these days. They do so because Warrington remains an important rail crossroads with as many main routes feeding into it as Crewe or Preston.

The former London and North Western Railway West Coast Main Line on its way from Euston to Carlisle is bisected by two east-west lines - what remains of the lesser LNWR Altrincham-Liverpool line passing directly underneath Bank Quay station, and the former Cheshire Lines Committee Manchester-Liverpool route crossing over the main line just north of Bank Quay and serving the town's Central station.

Warrington is also crossed by the main route from Manchester to Chester and North Wales. It feeds into the West Coast line three and a half miles north of Bank Quay at Winwick Junction via a connection from the Liverpool and Manchester Railway at Earlestown before heading off towards Chester from Acton Grange Junction, the south end of the Warrington rail complex.

Ever since the dawn of railways, Warrington has enjoyed a key position on the network, especially when it comes to freight.

For centuries, even as a small market town, it has been an important centre of communications, being the first point at which the River Mersey could be bridged.

Land travel, whether by foot, horse or coach, had to pass through Warrington while the river itself provided boat access to the open sea, to many coastal towns and for some distance inland.

These were good transport links in their day and later in the 18th Century, with the availability of cheap coal nearby, they encouraged a wide variety of industries to develop around a small harbour on the north bank of the river at Bank Quay. They included copper smelting, tanning, and the manufacture of glass, soap and chemicals.

These industries grew rapidly with the industrial revolution which also brought man made waterways, like the St. Helens Canal passing just west of the town. Steel became one of the biggest with several large plants including firms specialising in making wire, steel rope and tubes. Other big industries were chemicals, aluminium, board and paper, and the manufacture of detergents and bleaches at the huge Joseph Crosfield's soap and chemical works next to Bank Quay station. Greenall's and Walker's breweries provided the refreshment while the energy came from one of Britain's biggest gas works.

Warrington attracted the railway at an early stage and even though its railway story began at the end of a branch line, it was not long before the town was on one of the country's first major trunk routes.

The branch line was the Warrington and Newton Railway, opened in July, 1831 and running 4.25 miles from the Liverpool and Manchester Railway at Newton Junction (Earlestown) to Dallam Lane, just short of Warrington market place. It is said that the first tickets were sold at the Three Pigeons pub. The new railway included a short goods branch to Liverpool Road, just short of Bank Quay. Three locomotives designed by Robert Stephenson, the line's engineer - *Warrington, Vulcan and Newton* - worked the first trains. Through the L&M and the Wigan Branch Railway, opened in 1832 from Parkside, east of Earlestown, to Wigan, Warrington had direct links to the North West's three biggest industrial centres - Liverpool, Manchester and Wigan.

Warrington did not stay at the end of a branch line for long. Within a few years, the famous Grand Junction Railway from Birmingham was under construction. Running via Crewe, it was a vital link in the creation of the national rail network. Approaching Warrington it crossed the Mersey by a sandstone bridge known as Twelve Arches to meet the Warrington and Newton head-on at Liverpool Road. There a new station was established in place of Dallam Lane which continued to serve coal depots and private sidings until the late 1960s. Opening on 4th July, 1837, the Grand Junction not only gave Warrington

The London and North Western Railway opened Bank Quay station in 1868. This was how it looked from the south in the 1930s. Since then the far left platform has been extended, the platform buildings and canopy on the left modernised in the early 1960s, and the water tank on the right removed. Dominating the left is Crosfield's soap works and beyond the station is Liverpool Road bridge, the site of the previous station. *(Lens of Sutton)*

fast and direct transport to major centres in the south for the first time but, via the W&N(which it bought in 1835) and Liverpool and Manchester, created the first main line between Liverpool, Birmingham and London, a role it fulfilled until opening of the present route through Runcorn in 1869.

Next on the scene was the Birkenhead, Lancashire and Cheshire Junction Railway (later renamed the Birkenhead Railway) which opened the Chester line in December, 1853. Other railways were approaching too, from the east and west. The St. Helens Canal and Railway company, part owned by Warrington brewers Greenalls and banker William Parr, was building a branch from Widnes. It opened as far as a temporary terminus at White Cross, just west of Bank Quay, in February, 1853.

The SHCR was to join the BLCJR at Arpley but the BLCJR stopped short at Walton Junction. This not only left the SHCR high and dry but the BLCJR itself was at the mercy of the LNWR, the Grand Junction's ruthless and aquisitive successor, whose track it had to use to reach Warrington.

Coming in from the east like the cavalry, however, was the Warrington and Altrincham

Junction Railway(renamed the Warrington and Stockport after securing powers for an extension to Stockport). After some delay in completing the bridge over the river at Wilderspool, the Warrington and Stockport opened throughout on 1st May, 1854 to form a junction with the SHCR and establish the so-called Low Level line. As well as a joint W&S/SHCR station at Arpley, housing the W&S headquarters, the line included Warrington area stations at Latchford, Sankey Bridges and Fidlers Ferry & Penketh. The W&S was operated by the Manchester, Sheffield and Lincolnshire Railway, but the Great Northern also worked through to Walton Junction while the LNWR was granted access to Manchester

Some changes in ownership then followed, one giving the Great Western Railway a direct line into Warrington. With the LNWR it jointly took over the Birkenhead Railway from Chester in 1860. Around the same time, the LNWR leased the W&S, and the SHCR in 1864, giving it a virtual monopoly of lines into Warrington. That same year the LNWR opened a new cut-off line from Winwick to Golborne so that its expresses could avoid the trek through Earlestown and Parkside. In

1868 it replaced Liverpool Road and Arpley stations with a new two-level station at Bank Quay - today's station - where the West Coast main line crosses over the Low Level, although a legal requirement forced it to reopen Arpley in 1871.

In 1865, the LNWR stopped the MSL using the Low Level, foreshadowing the end of its stranglehold on Warrington for the MSL, in partnership with the Great Northern and Midland railways was planning its own route from Manchester to Liverpool. Together they formed a joint railway called the Cheshire Lines Committee. The new line was designed for fast running and would effectively by-pass the centre of Warrington, although local pressure forced the committee to add a 2.5-mile loop through the town centre where it would serve a new Central station. The CLC, via the loop, was opened in the early 1870s and Central station on 1st August, 1873. The originally planned direct line opened for freight and non-stop passenger trains in 1883, completing Warrington's main line network.

Towards the end of the 19th century came one more project, this time requiring major line deviations and the construction of substantial new bridges. Nowadays such things happen for the benefit of motorways but this was a new waterway - the Manchester Ship Canal which would take ocean-going vessels straight to the heart of one of Britain's most important industrial regions.

No longer would cargo be trans-shipped to and from trains at Liverpool or Birkenhead for the Manchester leg of the journey. The railways would lose traffic so they did not welcome having to step aside to let the canal through. They did all they could to protect their interests and delay the canal's opening.

The LNWR quite rightly objected to swing bridges where the canal bisected the Crewe, Chester and Low Level lines, especially if canal traffic had priority, and eventually persuaded the canal company to use fixed bridges. But these needed to be high enough for ships to pass under so the railways approaching them had to be rebuilt on embankments rising to great heights. These bridges were built at Acton Grange to carry the Crewe and Chester lines on a single structure, and at Latchford, where the Low Level line became anything but low level.

A fresh station was needed on the new alignment at Latchford, while the Chester line was diverted to a new junction with the Crewe line at Acton Grange. Walton Junction, where the two lines previously diverged, was renamed Walton Old Junction. A new bridge was needed to carry the raised Crewe line over the Mersey and new points

The Derby Works-built class 115 4-car suburban diesel multiple units were masters of the Cheshire Lines passenger services for 25 years since replacing steam in 1960.
One of them, with car No. M51856 nearest the camera, leaves Warrington Central with a Liverpool to Manchester service on 25the August, 1975. The goods yard is on the left and a class 108 waits in the carriage sidings. *(Gordon Coltas)*

The heavy steelwork of the Acton Grange bridge over the Manchester Ship Canal provides adequate support for an ex-LNWR 0-8-0 from Oldham Lees as it leaves Warrington with a southbound Through Freight in the late 1950s. These engines, notable for their absence of smokebox door numberplates, were routine power for goods trains around Warrington until the start of the 1960s. *(P. Norton collection)*

called Walton New Junction were installed between the canal and river bridges.

The scheme had its compensations for the railways though. The canal generated new freight traffic to and from industries setting up along its banks and the MSC laid its own line along the north bank linking factories and wharves to the main lines. The old alignment at Latchford and the stump of the old Chester line from Walton Old Junction to the canal were retained to provide connections between the LNWR and the MSC Railway. The stump of the Chester line south of the canal was kept as refuge sidings known as the Lay Bye. In the Warrington area, the MSC Railway served a creosoting works producing railway sleepers and telegraph poles, a plant making copper-lined tubes and boiler mountings, the MSC's own brick works, an aluminium works, a coal wharf for Haydock

Collieries and Wigg Brothers chemical works at Old Quay, west of Acton Grange. The MSCR also had its own engine shed and workshops at Latchford, and another shed for the Acton Grange end at Chester Road.

The Low Level line realignment also enabled some congested level crossings to be replaced by bridges but it was 1956 before the busiest, Chester Road at Wilderspool, was replaced.

The canal opened on 1st January, 1894 and for 70-80 years Warrington enjoyed relative stability on the railway front, hosting just about every kind of traffic. This covered everything from crack West Coast expresses like the Royal Scot, and the streamlined Coronation Scot of the 1930s, to the night-time mail and sleeper trains which raced through non-stop, or the Irish boat trains, holiday excursions and commuter 'Club' trains of the Manchester-North Wales route.

The CLC carried an intensive passenger service, including expresses between Liverpool Central, Manchester Central and destinations east of the Pennines, plus a Liverpool - Harwich boat train. Fast commuter trains scuttled between Manchester and Liverpool at a pace equalling and sometimes bettering the Trans-Pennine expresses on the main route through Earlestown.

The line brought Eastern Region engines deep into London Midland territory.

Local trains ran via the Low Level between Liverpool Lime Street or Runcorn, Bank Quay and Manchester Oxford Road. Often push-pull, they were worked by elegant old LNWR 2-4-2Ts such as 46603, 54, 88 and 701, and later by Stanier and Ivatt 2-6-2Ts like 41210, 11, 13, 17 and 88. Similar trains ran between Bank Quay and St. Helens, and Manchester Exchange or Bolton Great Moore Street via Leigh and Tyldesley.

Round the clock goods activity involved everything, from fast express freights to factory trips and lumbering coal trains, many from collieries around Wigan to the ship canal loading staithes at Partington, a move which required reversal at Walton Old Junction to reach the Low Level line.

The Low Level carried much freight between centres east of the Pennines and the chemical plants of Widnes and the docks at Garston and Liverpool. Export coal came from Yorkshire pits via the Sheffield-Manchester Woodhead line while bananas were among cargoes going back east. Many trains stopped at Arpley Junction or Bank Quay low level platforms to take water or change crews.

Being mainly a passenger railway, the CLC carried less freight but plenty used the avoiding line while Warrington Central had a big goods depot, the disused warehouse still proclaiming its joint ownership by the Great Central(the MSL's new name from 1899), the GN and Midland railways in 1996.

Warrington developed all the necessary facilities for marshalling, crewing and powering trains. Groups of sidings were established at Winwick Quay, Dallam, Froghall, Arpley and Walton Old Junction. There were also exchange sidings with the MSC Railway at Latchford and a large collection of sidings east of Central station where much of the traffic was generated by Ryland's wire works.

The main locomotive shed was at Dallam, on the Down, or west, side of the main line opposite the junction with the Dallam Lane branch, and at a conglomeration of sidings with the CLC avoiding line going over the top on a long bridge. Dallam supplied mainly goods engines while a smaller sub-shed at Arpley housed tank engines for local passenger work. Engine sidings behind Central station were used to stable locomotives used for local workings.

Although outside the scope of this book, it is worth recalling that just a few miles north of Warrington was the distinguished Vulcan Foundry. Established by Warrington iron founder Charles Tayleur Earle with Robert Stephenson one of his partners, it built thousands of steam, diesel and electric locomotives for the whole world. They ranged from humble colliery shunters to big main line engines. One of its claims to fame was to have supplied India with a new locomotive every fortnight for 100 years, as well as turning out hundreds of War Department locomotives for the second world war effort and numerous Black Five 4-6-0s. From 1955, under English Electric ownership, it built many diesel and electric locomotives for British Railways - among them the celebrated Deltics and the class 40s and 50s which hauled WCML expresses right past its back door. The works had its own internal railway connected to the Winwick - Earlestown line, and between 1912 and 1965 its own station, called Vulcan Halt. It ceased building main line locomotives in 1969 but turned out industrial shunters for a few more years, concentrating finally on diesel power units.

Warrington escaped the savage cuts which swept the main line system but not without a lot of rationalisation. Sankey Bridges station closed on 26th September, 1949, Fidlers Ferry & Penketh on 2nd January, 1950, and Arpley, for the final time, on 15th September, 1958, the buildings and old W&S headquarters being demolished in the 1960s.

The Bolton trains went in 1954 and all other local services were axed during the 1960s. The Low Level lost all its regular passenger services except a Liverpool-York night mail, on 10th September, 1962. The mail was switched to the CLC on 4th January, 1965 and the Low Level became freight only but

The principal locomotive depot in Warrington was at Dallam. It was no beauty spot but as this picture shows was full of atmosphere, in fact the atmosphere was always visible. BR class 9F 2-10-0 No. 92028, formerly equipped with a Franco-Crosti boiler, goes on shed as a variety of other goods and mixed traffic engines await their next turns of duty.

for summer Saturday excursions, especially between Yorkshire and North Wales, routed via Stockport, Arpley Junction and the Chester line. The CLC line service was restructured into an hourly pattern of Manchester-Liverpool diesel multiple units interspersed by local stopping trains.

Diesels replaced steam which hung on to the bitter end in 1968. The main line's magnificent Coronation Pacifics were ignominiously relegated to freight and parcels duties before being wiped out in 1964. From 4th May, 1970 all daytime expresses through Bank Quay were taken over by new 2,700hp class 50 diesels built at Vulcan Foundry. They superseded the English Electric Type 4s(class 40s) and Brush Type 4s(class 47s) which had themselves replaced steam a few years before. The 50s generally double-headed Anglo-Scottish trains and single-headed Blackpool, Carlisle and Barrow trains.

Freight was declining but in 1971 the massive coal-fired Fiddlers Ferry power station came on stream. Designed to receive 4 million tons of railborn coal a year, it brought new life to the Low Level line. The station was fed by 1,000-ton plus trains bringing coal from Yorkshire and the East Midlands.

In 1985, the 90 year-old Latchford bridge needed expensive repairs which could not be justified and the whole line east of Warrington was shut on 7th July. Around 20 daily freight trains were rerouted, including those serving Fiddlers Ferry which began to

approach Warrington from the Earlestown direction, requiring reversal at Walton Old and Arpley junctions. Both the new and original lines were retained between Arpley Junction and Latchford for reversing the coal trains. They were still running this way in late 1996 but coal was also being imported through Liverpool docks.

In the early 1970s the West Coast Main Line through Warrington to Glasgow was electrified. The work was preceeded by resignalling which saw all the manual WCML signal boxes around Warrington replaced by one new power box at Bank Quay controlling 62 route miles(145 miles of track). With its 64ft console, computerised train describers and remote-control interlockings as far away as Wigan and St. Helens Junction, the new box was commissioned in October, 1972. The electrification was officially completed on 7th May, 1974 but by early 1973 electric locomotives were hauling freight and parcels trains into Warrington yards, and passenger trains to Preston by May.

As this Railway Memories went to press, renewal of the 1970s trains and infrastructure was eagerly awaited, as was the introduction of international passenger services via the Channel Tunnel.

Bank Quay is still an important stop for InterCity trains to Scotland, London, the West Country and the South Coast. The Manchester-North Wales expresses still run, albeit with Sprinter and class 158 DMUs. In

After being displaced by diesels from top link express duties, the ex-LMS class 8P Pacifics were relegated to freight and parcels. No. 46237 *City of Bristol* heads past Dallam with an Oxley(Wolverhampton) to Carlisle fitted freight in 1963. (*Trevor Rowe*)

1994 local trains returned to Bank Quay in the shape of a Liverpool-Ellesmere Port/Chester service.

In the mid-1980s the faster CLC DMUs were replaced by loco-hauled expresses between Liverpool, Sheffield, Hull or East Anglia. In 1989 it became the main Trans-Pennine route, carrying the Liverpool-Newcastle expresses - and a reintroduced train to Harwich. The loco-hauled trains were quickly replaced by new 158s and Sprinters and today Warrington Central has as good a service as ever with direct trains to such places as Sunderland, Leeds, York, Newcastle, Nottingham and Norwich.

In 1996, the surviving yards at Arpley and Walton Old Junction were still busy while the site of Arpley engine shed could be seen holding a dozen or more locomotives.

Alas, while plenty of freight still passes through, virtually all of Warrington's originating traffic has disappeared. The factories and steelworks which generated so much rail traffic have closed or switched to road. The Monks Hall rolling mills, connected to the Low Level line west of Bank Quay on a site which until the 1930s made everything from steel tubes to bedsteads, closed in 1986, end-ing the town's 120-year steelmaking industry, although some wire firms live on. In 1996 the only freight terminal is at Dallam, handling steel and general goods.

Having past into the ownership of the London Midland and Scottish Railway in 1923(jointly with the London and North Eastern in the case of the CLC) and British Railways London Midland Region in 1948, Warrington's railways are now being returned to an even more complex array of private companies as BR is sold off in bits. Infrastructure and signalling control now come under Railtrack and most freight and mail trains are run by the American-owned English, Welsh and Scottish Railway. Passenger services, still run by BR companies in late 1996, were due to be franchised out to private bidders soon after.

Despite all the changes which have taken place since the last Black Fives and 9Fs puffed away from Dallam shed, Bank Quay station and Slutcher's Lane bridge across Arpley Junction can still be a magnet for those observing and recording the railway scene. In Railway Memories No. 9 we celebrate the foresight of those who did just that in the 1950s and 60s.

Above: The end was nigh for the Coronation Pacifics when this picture was taken in 1964 but No. 46251 *City of Nottingham* looked in fine fettle while racing an Up express over Winwick Junction and towards Warrington..

THE FIVE GOLDEN MILES

Below: Winwick Junction in the mid-1950s before the footbridge was removed.
Royal Scot 4-6-0 No. 46168 *The Girl Guide* joins the original Warrington and Newton Railway route from Earlestown while travelling at speed along the main line from Wigan with a southbound express. Vulcan Foundry is prominent on the skyline and the St. Helens Canal on the left.
(R.S.Carpenter Photos)

Above: Looking south from the overbridge at Winwick Junction as a Stanier Black Five 4-6-0 accelerates northwards with an express goods.

Below: Between Winwick Junction and Winwick Quay, Patricroft - based BR Standard class 5 4-6-0 No. 73140, one of the batch fitted with Caprotti valve gear, has charge of a lightweight 1960s express from Manchester Exchange while passing the spot where the Winwick Hospital Railway went off to the right.

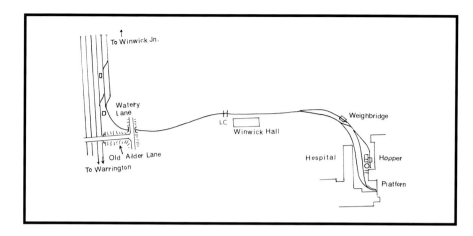

Left: The Winwick Hall hospital railway in 1963/64.
(Not to scale)

South of Winwick Junction, a short private branch line, around half a mile long, left a pair of exchange sidings connected to the Up Slow line and ran right into the Lancashire County Mental Hospital at Winwick Hall.

The line passed under the junction of Watery Lane and Old Alder Lane and was used for delivering coal to the hospital boilers which provided hot water for the heating and laundry. At the hospital were an unloading hopper, a weighbridge and a run-round loop. Movements between the exchange sidings and the Up Slow were controlled by a ground frame.

The main line company's engines worked the branch, usually with three or four wagons. In BR days it was a regular job for one of the 2-6-2Ts off the St. Helens passenger service.

The branch fell out of use in the early 1960s and although the 1964 Ordnance Survey sheet shows it intact it must have been disused by then. The picture opposite, taken between 1964 and 1967, shows the track gone and the formation destroyed.

In late 1996, the old trackbed beyond the bridge under Watery Lane is remarkably well preserved. The bridge itself has been filled in but wooden parapet fencing survives.

Below: The lattice footbridge at Winwick Quay was a popular haunt for young spotters with the bonus of frog spawn from surrounding marsh land and low flying American Army planes landing at the nearby Burtonwood air base. Passing underneath with an Up goods in the 1960s was ex-LMS Black Five 4-6-0 No. 45185.
The bridge was rebuilt for the 1970s electrification and in 1996 is the only way of identifying this once busy railway location.

Above: More menial work for a Coronation. No. 46250 *City of Lichfield* passes Winwick Quay on the Down Slow with a northbound van train. In the late 1960s/early 70s the weight bar spindle on these signals was so worn that when the signalman returned the signal to danger after passing a freight, one of the weights lodged against the one next to it and left the signal slightly 'off.' The driver of a following passenger train took the signal to be clear and ran into the back of the goods.

Below: WD 2-8-0 No. 90178 confidently rolls a coal train along the Up Fast and overtakes 'Crab ' 2-6-0 No. 42841 on the Up Slow while passing Winwick Quay signal box on 30th July, 1963. No. 44522 is the 4F 0-6-0 waiting in the yard with a ballast train.

SHORT MEMORIES

5.10.57: Stanier class 3 2-6-2Ts 40125/56 transferred to Dallam.

Autumn 1958: Closure of Manchester London Road station for electrification work means that Liverpool-Bank Quay Low Level - Manchester services are worked by DMUs turned back at Oxford Road or Warwick Road.

23.4.60: Unrebuilt Patriot 4-6-0s 45501 *St Dunstan's,* 45511 *Isle of Man,* and 45546 *Fleetwood* transferred to Dallam.

May/June 1960: The turntable at Dallam shed is closed for repairs so engines have to turn on Earlestown triangle.

June 1960: New 'Peak' Type 4 diesel D9 *Snowdon* passes Warrington while crew training between Crewe and Edge Hill.

Sept 1960: Ex-Midland 3F 0-6-0 No. 43410 is allocated to Dallam. So is Caprotti and roller bearings-fitted Black Five 44750, and unrebuilt Patriots 45524 *Blackpool* and 45544. Warrington's Patriots later find regular work on the Chester-Birkenhead line freights.

Above: One of Warrington's local services, the stopper from St. Helens Shaw Street (now Central) passes Winwick Quay with a two-car Derby-built diesel multpile unit doing the honours. This service was withdrawn on 14th June, 1965.

Below: Not the sort of thing you saw everyday at Winwick Quay! Ex-Caledonian Railway 4-2-2 No. 123, restored by BR's Scottish Region for working special trains, heads towards Warrington in the early 1960s.

Bellcode Books proprietor Stephen Chapman had a brief but memorable encounter with steam-age Warrington on 31st July, 1963 while travelling on the Manchester - Holyhead boat train.
"As the train was standing in the back platform at Bank Quay station I heard a whistle screaming continuously. I scrambled to the window just in time to see Britannia No. 70025 Western Star rushing through non-stop at the head of a southbound express. The noise was terrific.
"The only time I had seen an express racing along like that with the whistle blowing was in films. Now I had experienced it for real and I would never forget it".

15

Above: Black Five 4-6-0 No. 44737 passes an unusually empty Winwick Quay yard while heading an Up West Coast express, possibly from Blackpool since that was 44737's home shed at the time.

Below: Everything happened at once when this picture was taken from Winwick Quay footbridge. Black Five 44689 was on an Up express as Stanier 2-6-0 42970 went north with an express goods and a BR Standard class 4 4-6-0 shunted ballast wagons. The first wagon in the goods is a sludge tender carrying lime scale removed from a water softening plant . It could have come from the softener at Moore troughs, south of Warrington, which had a siding for loading such wagons.

Right: Stockport-based Black Five No. 44755 was no beauty but she made a fascinating sight in 1963 while putting a train together under the supervision of the Winwick Quay shunter, pole in hand.

44755 was one of three Black Fives modified in 1948 with Caprotti valve gear, Timken roller bearings and double chimney. It would be interesting to hear the reaction should someone suggest rebuilding one of today's many preserved Black Fives to look like this.

Below: One of Dallam's 4F 0-6-0s, No. 44219, ambles along the Up Slow with a fair load of coal. Today, the site of Winwick Quay sidings is occupied by light industrial units but the four track main line remains busy.

Contrasts on the southern approach to Winwick Quay.
Above: Coronation class 4-6-2 No. 46225 *Duchess of Gloucester* puts on a brave face while forging north towards Winwick Quay with a van train in 1964.

Below: In 1963 few enthusiasts wanted to even look at trains like this let alone photograph them, but in the 1990s even the sight of these Birmingham Railway Carriage and Wagon (class 104) diesel multiple units will tug more than a few heart strings. They look picturesque indeed while forming a North Wales to Manchester additional service on 10th August.

SHORT MEMORIES

10.2.61: Class 8P Pacific No. 46226 *Duchess of Norfolk* fails at Warrington while working the 6.15am Carlisle-Crewe. After receiving attention at Dallam shed and turning on Earlestown triangle, she heads back home with the 10am Walton Old Junction - Carlisle goods.

Sept,1961: Midland Railway 3F 0-6-0 No. 43257 is alocated to Dallam along with BR Standard class 2MT 2-6-2T No. 84024.

18.5.63: Black Five No. 45156 *Ayrshire Yeomanry* allocated to to Dallam shed.

Above: Britannias were rarely seen on the West Coast Main Line until being transferred en- mass from the Eastern Region in 1963. After the end of the Coronations in 1964 they became the route's only Pacific power and were prolific performers through Warrington to the end of steam.
No. 70011 *Hotspur*, recently transferred from March to Carlisle Kingmoor, approaches Winwick Quay with a Down express freight conveying another of those sludge tenders.

Below: The new development which now fills the lineside between Winwick Quay and Warrington gets under way in the distance as Black Five 4-6-0 45403 cuts through a stiff breeze with a Chester to Manchester stopper.

Above: Blackpool class 6P Jubilee 4-6-0 45584 *North West Frontier* rolls a southbound 1960s express past Warrington's infamous gas works and through the expanse of railway that was Dallam.

Below: The Great Western Railway had access to Warrington but this would not have been how it intended its trains to get there. Class 57XX 0-6-0 pannier tank No. 9753, formerly of Tyseley shed, Birmingham, is being dragged to its doom past Dallam by a Black Five, its destination the Central Wagon Company's scrapheap in Wigan.
On the right are the gas works sidings complete with coal, coke and tar wagons as well as mountainous stockpiles of coal or coke. Howard's scrap yard siding goes off to the left.
Both these pictures were taken by Trevor Rowe from Dallam Branch Sidings signal box when he worked there as a signal lad. The view he had then may have been far from pretty but it ouzed railway interest.

Above: Harry Wilde and his fireman wave for the camera while heading north past Dallam box with a Froghall to Bamfurlong(Wigan) goods in about 1964. Their engine is Dallam Jubilee 45580 *Burma*. *(Trevor Rowe)*

Below: A workstained 4F on a coal train was a familar sight at Dallam in the early 1960s, hardly worth a second glance but how we would revel in a scene like this today. No. 44377 passes Dallam with Longford's wire works on the right while trundling its train along the Up Fast line. Dallam men called the 4Fs 'Plus Fours.'

Britannias and a little bit more at Dallam.

Above: No. 70035 *Rudyard Kipling* races along the Up Fast with the 6.38am Workington to Euston in 1964. Just above 70035's smokebox is a Sentinel steam locomotive which shunted in the gas works. The last Britannia was ousted from BR in 1968 but some Sentinels, which featured vertical boilers, gearboxes and chain drive, worked on in industry until the early 1980s.

Below: It is 1965 and signalman Eddie Chadwick watches from Dallam Branch Sidings box as spotless 70054 *Dornoch Firth* comes off shed. *(Both Trevor Rowe)*

Tragedy struck in the early 1960s after colour light signalling was installed at Bank Quay.

The Liverpool Edge Hill crew of a northbound express goods thought the new signals meant 'right away' and missed the old semaphores approaching Dallam. As they accelerated north, a light engine from Dallam shed was crossing to the Up side.

When the Dallam men realised what was about to happen they tried to reverse their engine out of the way but the driving wheels spun helplessly and the goods rammed into them mid-way over the Down Fast crossing.

The damage was severe and, sadly, the Warrington fireman was so badly scalded by escaping steam that he later died.

Above: With driver Ned Archer on the footplate, 4F 44294 rests while shunting what is probably Target 88 trip at Dallam sidings. The routine for this working was to shunt the yard and then stop for their butties. Alongside the gas works, this was not the most celubrious setting for lunch. *(Trevor Rowe)*

Below: 'Crab' 2-6-0 42942 sets back past Dallam box while going on shed after working a Birkenhead to Froghall goods. The Dallam Lane branch goes left through the bridge, beyond which are Dallam sidings and the Dallam Forge and Bewsey steelworks. *(Trevor Rowe)*

23

Above: Final journey for WDs 90181, 90314 and 90541 being dragged to the scrapyard past Dallam by an 8F 2-8-0. Such trains of 'scrappers' with brake vans were all too common in the 1960s. When there was no brake van a man rode in the last engine to put the brake on if anything went wrong.

Below: One of the Jubilees rebuilt as class 7P, No. 45736 *Phoenix* makes a stirring sight while heading a Down parcels past Dallam box in 1965. *(Both Trevor Rowe)*

Above: Dallam in all its glory as Black Five 45372 passes the loco shed. Wagons on the far left mark the Dallam Lane branch, while Dallam sidings fill the centre and the English Steel company's works the centre background. The CLC avoiding line goes left to right over the top.

Below: Looking from the other side during 1964 as Jubilee No. 45689 *Ajax* hauls a BR/Sulzer Type 2 diesel(class 24) southbound between Dallam Sidings and the shed.

Dallam motive power depot was coded 8B in BR's Liverpool district. It consisted of a straight shed with ten roads, a coaling stage with overhead water tank and a turntable. At the coaling stage, the coal was shovelled by hand out of wagons on a raised siding and on to a conveyor which took it to the engines. The shed was re-roofed in 1957 and the number of roads reduced to nine.

Dallam was always primarily a steam depot providing engines for freight and local passenger work and shunters were the only diesels allocated there apart from a BR/Sulzer Type 2 for a short time just before closure.

It closed completely with the end of steam there on 2nd October, 1967 and in 1996 a modern factory building of almost exact size occupied the site. It is said that the shed walls remain, encased by the new building.

Above: Like Dr. Who's Tardis, Dallam shed seemed bigger on the inside than the outside. Here, the wooden smoke troughs and glazed roof impose a cathedral atmosphere cutting the huge bulk of 9F 2-10-0s Nos. 92116 and 92013 down to size as they stand proudly alongside pioneer Black Five No. 44658.

LOCOMOTIVES ALLOCATED TO WARRINGTON DALLAM

September, 1950

Fowler 3P 2-6-2T: 40042; Stanier 4P 2-6-4T: 42606/7; Johnson 3F 0-6-0: 43237/82/3/314/29/89/ 98/615/8/57; 5MT 4-6-0: 44897/5001/32/5/72/109/49/96/252/5/305/21/8/54/70; Patriot 7P 4-6-0: 45521 *Rhyl;* 1P 2-4-2T: 46603/54/88/701; 3F 0-6-0T: 47268/352/76/87/591/603/52/4/7; 8F 2-8-0: 48366/436/466/9/664/89; 7F 0-8-0: 49008/119/247; Aspinall 2P 2-4-2T: 50697/703/5; Aspinall 3F 0-6-0: 52088; Hughes 3F 0-6-0: 52598/608. Total: 57

July, 1962

2MT 2-6-2T: 41210/1/3/7/88; 3F 0-6-0: 43240/57/82/615/57; 4F 0-6-0 44061/3/219/32/7/9/356/84/494/ 522/4/89; 5MT 4-6-0: 45035/150/271/321/8/43/81/414/95; Jubilee 6P 4-6-0: 45583 *Assam,* 45638 *Zanzibar,* 45655 *Keith,* 45671 *Prince Rupert;* 3F 0-6-0T 47362/406/603/54/7; 8F 2-8-0: 48094/106/268/326/631/509/12/54/715; 2MT 2-6-2T: 84000/1; 170hp 0-4-0 diesel: D2864/5; 350hp 0-6-0diesel: D3851/12070/5/6/8/100. Total 59.

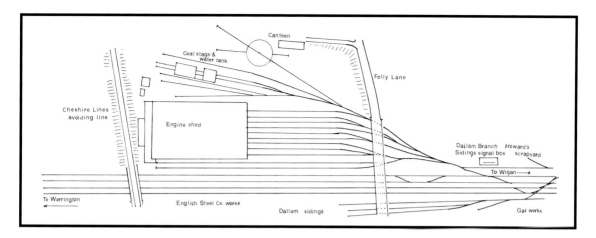

Above: The layout at Dallam shed, as it was in 1964. *(Not to scale)*

Right: By the time this picture was taken, the staple motive power for local passenger services through Warrington Bank Quay was Dallam's Ivatt class 2MT 2-6-2Ts. Nos. 41217 and 41211 sit on Dallam shed, facing Folly lane bridge, with less work to do since closure of the Low Level line passenger service in 1962.

Bottom: This engine is still working in 1996, on the Severn Valley Railway, and is the only one of its type left.
Ivatt class 4MT 2-6-0 No. 43106 was a Heaton Mersey engine when photographed parked outside Dallam shed in 1964.

The normal position of the shed outlet signal is Clear. Drivers of engines ready to leave the Shed must stop at the signal and telephone their destination and title of train to be worked to the signalman at Dallam Branch Sidings box and then wait instructions. When the signal is placed to danger for an engine to enter the shed, shunting movements must cease and drivers must bring their engines to a stand behind the signal. *London Midland Region Sectional Appendix, 1962.*

Above: This was the breathtaking sight that awaited the eager enthusiast pearing over the wall of Folly Lane bridge in steam days. When the young Trevor Rowe took this shot, early in 1963, Dallam's ex-Midland Railway 3F 0-6-0s still had a few months' life left in them while Ivatt 2-6-2T No. 41211, heading the line-up, still had some work to do. Ex-LMS class 3F 0-6-0T No. 47594 is the shed pilot and the Cheshire Lines avoiding line forms the skyline in the centre of the picture.

Below: Few pictures capture the character of steam-age railway-men better than this one. Like these Dallam men in the mess room, they worked hard in conditions which would not be tolerated today yet always kept their dignity and pride in the job.

SHORT MEMORIES

5.9.64: Yellow stripe Jubilee 4-6-0 45600 *Bermuda* passes through Warrington dragging electric loco E3065 and its Liverpool to Euston express.

5.9.64: A job lot of Black Five 4-6-0s transferred from Blackpool to Dallam consists of 44730/1/819/930/5078/238/56/ 303/436.

20.2.65: A football special from Wellington, Shrewsbury and Chester to Leeds for the FA Cup fifth round passes through Bank Quay hauled by Britannia 4-6-2 No. 70053 *Moray Firth*.

Above: This picture and the one opposite give a good general view of Dallam shed yard as seen from Folly Lane. Uncharacteristically clean 8F No. 48637 uses the turntable while a Jubilee sits in the 'coal hole' and 3F 0-6-0 tank and tender engines on No. 9 shed road. *(Trevor Rowe)*

Below: Dallam Jubilee No. 45563 *Australia*, begrimed, festooned with old lamps and dumped by the coal stage attracts symapthy from a young admirer. On the right is the raised road from which coal wagons were manually unloaded. The coal stage was known to shed staff as the 'Sputnik.'

Above: The car completes a trul;y delightful scene while keeping company with a pair of Black Fives deep inside Dallam shed. It is standing on the site of No.10 road which was probably removed when the shed was re-roofed in 1957.

Left: Dallam's class 3F 0-6-0s, like 43615, had reached the end of the line by the time this view was taken and were dumped on the scrap line which ran along the outside of the shed next to the main line. The siding was known locally as 'Abyssinia', possibly because when an engine went down there it did not come out again under its own steam and it was a case of "A'll be seein' yer."

Above: Two classics come face to face at Dallam turntable - 9F 2-10-0 No. 92124 and an early 1960s Hillman Minx.

Below: One of just four named Stanier Black Fives, No. 45154 *Lanarkshire Yeomanry* pays Dallam shed a visit in 1964 during which time it had spells allocated to Wigan, Newton Heath and Carnforth.

Two gloriously grimy views at Dallam shed.
Above: Encrusted grime and missing number plates render this BR Standard class 5 4-6-0 and 9F 2-10-0 anonymous as they stand amid the debris of steam.

Below: The morning sun brings a bit of a shine to 8F 2-8-0 No. 48736 as it boils up alongside Speke Junction 9F No. 92104.

Peter Kelly, editor of the popular monthly magazine Steam Railway, spent many happy childhood years observing the 1950s Warrington railway scene.

The West Coast main line was a big attraction and Winwick Quay was one of the nearest spots to where he lived.

"To get there, we walked across a field, then along a bridle path to the Wigan road. There we bought Penny Arrow bars from a little shop in the downstairs room of a brick house and took them to the footbridge, along a path across what was then marshy ground.

"I saw my only streamlined Coronation Pacific from that bridle path. I was only about three and it was quite a way off. I just remember the shape - a big black thing.

"We went to Winwick Quay as much for the planes as trains. The end of the runway at Burtonwood American air base was just half a mile away and all these American planes like Flying Fortresses and Dakotas would come in to land, just yards above our heads.

"We always tried to get there in time for a train we called the '10 O'clocker.' This was in 1954/55 and it must have been a Carlisle train. It was always a Britannia, one of those named after Firths. Britannias were real rarites then so this was very exciting.

"One evening in 1957 crowds of people turned out to see what the newspapers reported as a new eight-coach high speed train. I joined them at Winwick Quay and saw the first northbound Caledonian go through on time at 7.5pm. *City of London* worked it one way and *City of Glasgow* the other.

"That year, I also saw the first class 20 diesel coming from Vulcan Foundry. I thought it looked beautiful. bright green with white discs and the cab where it should be. Another time I saw one of the first North British 'Warships' in the D600 series.

"From 1960/61 came the sad and relentless scrap trains - four or five engines, perhaps Midland 4-4-0s. Even the engine pulling them, possibly a 4F, seemed on its last legs."

Sometimes Peter joined the spotters gathering in the sun trap that was Bank Quay horse dock, behind huge advertising hoardings overlooking South End carriage sidings.

"Expresses passed Bank Quay at a hell of arate and when the Royal Scot came through with the two diesels, 10000 and 10001 the effect was explosive. They really rattled, like

A sight from the 60s to savour - Stanier 2-6-0 No. 42959 has steam to spare while pacing along the Down Fast with a Crewe to Bamfurlong goods in 1964. (*Trevor Rowe*)

a present day unsilenced diesel.

"Some of the heavy Scotland-London trains had three of four six-wheel milk tankers on the back which swung about alarmingly if they came through at anything over 60mph."

Little did Peter Kelly know it but his future career was probably decided by one experience at Bank Quay when he was 13.

"It was a miserable, drizzly day. Princess Royal class *Queen Maude* came in and stopped. When she set off again, she lost her footing and started slipping badly, she stopped and slipped again, stopped again and slipped again, and went on like that until she disappeared into the murk well beyond the Mersey bridge. It was just the inspiration I needed for a school essay which turned out to be the best in our class.

"The Up Perth to London train was 16-17 coaches hauled by a Princess. If no Princess was available, it would be a Royal Scot always piloted by a Carlisle 2P 4-4-0.

"When we had spotted everything worth seeing on the West Coast Main Line we turned to the Cheshire Lines - it was magic to see locos which had numbers starting with a 6.

"We followed a path to the footbridge at Padgate Junction. The path went along the perimeter fence of the RAF training camp and on Saturday mornings the air was filled with the crackle of rifle fire from the ranges.

"It was a great place between 4 and 7pm on weekdays with all the commuter trains. The tank engines pulling them could really accelerate from Padgate. Goods trains coming from the avoiding line nearly always had to stop at signals by the bridge. The loop was very busy and on the avoiding line you waited no longer than 40-45 minutes for a goods.

"On the avoiding line we saw O4 and WD 2-8-0s which echoed against the backs of the terraced houses as they clanked slowly above Orford Park on long, unfitted goods and mineral trains. When D11 4-4-0 *Jutland* came along with a short goods one day in 1953 it was my first ever LNER namer.

"One Grand National day I was in Withers Avenue when an immaculate K3 2-6-0 with blood and custard coaches went along the avoiding line bound for Aintree. Grand National day saw four or five specials from the Eastern Region using the avoiding line.

"Passenger trains were rare on the avoiding line but in the late 1950s an afternoon Liverpool-Hull express went that way - a class 4 tank and eight coaches.

"One Saturday we went on a special Cheap Day excursion to Southport which we had to catch at Padgate because it did not stop at Central. It had a 'Crab' up front and it was the only time I travelled on the avoiding line.

"Sometimes we went spotting at Padgate station, a really peaceful place which has hardly changed, except that in those days there was always someone about in uniform. Today there are no staff at all."

Shrouded in clouds of steam, 9F 2-`0-0 No. 92055 comes under the Cheshire Lines route from Warrington Central at Froghall with a short freight on 3rd March, 1967. The arch accommodates a long headshunt known as the 'Gullet.'

Small industrial engines like this delightful little 1899-built 0-4-0T at Dallam Forge on 22nd March, 1958, once shunted many of the works yards in Warrington. The loco is standing on the tracks that ran between the CLC and Dallam sidings with the West Coast Main Line in a cutting behind it.

Dallam Forge continued using diesels until closure in 1983. *(Hugh Davies)*

By 1973 there were just nine sites left in Warrington with their own locomotives, and not all were still in use.

Howley power station: Three Fowler 0-4-0 diesels to shunt coal drops at Wilderspool feeding a conveyor taking coal to the power station on the other side of the Mersey. **Dallam Forge** steelworks: three Yorkshire Engine 0-4-0 diesels on the internal network. **Monk's Hall** works: one Yorkshire and one Fowler. **Ryland-Whitecross Wire**: a Fowler 0-4-0 *Lance* at Dalton Bank works and Motorail 4-wheel petrol loco built in 1937 at Battersby Lane plant. **Joseph Brierley's** scrap yard: a Fowler 0-4-0 diesel. **Crosfield's** and **ICI's Wigg** works each had a Fowler 0-4-0 and the gas works a Ruston 4-wheeler, all disused.

In addition, the MSC Railway still allocated an engine to shunt the Laporte chemical works at Walton, while the Department of the Environment had standard and 2ft gauge Rustons on the large network at the former US Burtonwood air base.

Warrington private sidings, 1957

The 1957 British Transport Commission Handbook of Stations listed no less than 51 private siding connections in Warrington. Shown with main line access points, they were:

Joseph Brierley (Wilderspool)
British Aluminium(B. Quay/MSC)
British Ropes (Sankey Bridges)
Central Elect. Authority (Arpley)
Clare & Ridgeway (Sankey Bridges)
Crosfield's - Factory Lane Siding, Pochin's Sdg, Robinson's Sdg. (all at Bank Quay). Soap works Sdgs. (BQ Low Level), and Transporter Bridge (via Crosfield's High Sidings).
Dallam Lane Coal Co's depot
Dussek Bitumen & Taroleum (Greenall's branch, Wilderspool)
English Gelatine & Phosphate (MSCR Acton Grange)
Fairclough & Son (Low Level line)
Fletcher Russell (Wilderspool)
Garton's Siding (Arpley)
Greenall's Brewery (Wilderspool)
Greening & Son (Bank Quay-Winwick)
George Howard Ltd.(Dallam)
ICI Wigg works (MSCR Acton Grange)
Lancs County Mental Hospital, Winwick Hall Siding
Longford Wire (Dallam Lane)
MSCR, Acton Grange

Lancashire Steel Corp., Dallam Forge, Bewsey Forge and pumping station. (CLC and Dallam Lane)
MSC Stores & Engineers Dept. (Acton Grange)
Mersey White Lead (Sankey Bridges)
Monk's Hall steel works.
NCB, Lay Bye & timber yard
NCB, Tanner's Lane coal depot
R.A. Naylor (MSCR Acton Grange)
North Western Gas Board (Dallam)
Payne & Co (Monk's Hall)
Pendlebury & Co (Dallam Lane)
Richardson's Coal (Dallam Lane)
Richardson's Old Road (Latchford)
Rubery Owen (Sankey Bridges)
Rylands Wire, Battersby Lane & Dalton Bank factories (CLC)
J. Tennant (BQ-Winwick)
Thames Board (Arpley-Walton)
Walker's Brewery (Dallam Lane)
Warrington Light Castings(Arpley)
Warrington Slate (Arpley and Dallam Lane)
Warrington Union Workhouse Siding (CLC)
Whitecross Wire - New Ropery and wire rope Sidings (CLC)
Whitecross wireworks (Froghall)

The long headshunt known as 'The Gullet' ran all the way from South End sidings to beyond the CLC bridge at Froghall.

Until 1996 some old tank wagons were stored there which once carried heating oil from the carriage and wagon repair sidings, where they were loaded from road tankers, to some pre-fab offices at Arpley sidings.

Above: Fowler diesel shunters were to be found in several factory yards around Warrington until the 1980s. One nicely turned out example was 1940 vintage 22873 at Whitecross wire on 9th July, 1968. Looking south, Liverpool Road bridge and Froghall sidings are on the left. *(Adrian Booth).*

Below: The north end of Bank Quay station as seen from South End sidings on 2nd September, 1967. The 9F with the brake van is 92224, an English Electric Type 4 runs through light on the Down Fast while Black Five No. 45323 lurks behind the station. *(Peter Rose)*

Crosfield's had their own rail vans marked 'For the use of Joseph Crosfield & Son Ltd., Warrington". They could get 40 whenever they wanted.

Five or six vans would go in a warehouse for loading and be out again within the hour.

Above: A captivating moment at the north end of Bank Quay station's Down Fast platform on 2nd September, 1967. The steam era has less than a year left but grime encrusted Black Five No. 44933 has charge of the 09.10 Euston to Blackpool express. Liverpool Road bridge lies ahead and Warrington goods depot is just beyond it on the right. *(Peter Rose)*

Below: Moments after Peter Rose took the picture opposite, 45323 began heading north with its express goods. On the right is one of the warehouses where rail vans were loaded with detergents from Crosfield's soap works, now Lever Brothers.

Above: Crewe South's Black Five No. 44678 looks in good nick as it shunts container wagons in South End sidings during 1965. The horse dock, the local spotters' regular vantage point, is on the right while pigeon baskets litter the Bank Quay platform, left. Most of South End yard is now occupied by a car park and DIY superstore, just a couple of sidings remaining.

Below: Black Fives may have been ten-a-penny at Warrington but at least there were variations - Caprottis, namers and Carlisle-based 45081 with its self-weighing tender. It is seen behind Bank Quay station with a northbound express goods.

SHORT MEMORIES

1.2.65: DMUs replace steam on Manchester-North Wales services except for the 16.25 Holyhead-Manchester and 22.00 return boat trains. Trains handed over to DMUs include the 07.40 Llandudno-Manchester and 16.30 return 'Club' trains.

The 12.00 Manchester-Holyhead becomes a Derby Lightweight unit for the 124-mile, 4.5 hour journey, replacing an 8-coach steam train which included a buffet and parcels vans.

The DMUs are mostly already well worn 4-car class 104 and 2-car Metro-Cammell class 101 sets.

In 1957 Warrington Bank Quay passenger and goods stations could handle furniture vans, portable engines and machines on wheels, live-stock, horse boxes, cattle vans, carriages and motor cars. The goods depot had a fixed crane with a maximum lifting capacity of 10 tons.

Above: This picture may be far from perfect but it is well worth inclusion because of the memories it evokes for those who spent many happy hours of their youth at Bank Quay in the 1960s.
Young spotters flock round, some in hope of cabbing Aston-based Jubilee No. 45586 *Mysore* as it deals with an Up parcels train in 1962. The low level platform buildings can be glimpsed just to the right of the engine.

Below: Patriot 4-6-0 No. 45501 *St. Dunstan's* may be a bit grimy but still presents a wonderful sight while easing an express van train along the Up Fast through Bank Quay in March, 1961. By then a Carlisle Upperby engine, *St. Dunstan's* had just completed a short spell at Dallam. It was one of the first two Patriots, being rebuilt in 1930 from an LNWR 'Claughton.' (*B. Magilton / Colour-Rail*)

BANK QUAY WEEKDAY PASSENGER SERVICES 2.11.1959 - 12.6.1960

Departure Time	Train
Pass	9.5pm Euston-Glasgow *sleeper*
Pass	11.25pm Birmingham-Glasgow/
	Edinburgh Princes St. *sleeper*
Pass	10.40pm Euston-Perth sleeper
Pass	10.30pm Euston-Whitehaven
2.57am	10.55pm Euston-Blackpool N

Also Windermere MX/sleeping car to Corkickle

Pass	11.40pm Euston-Glasgow St. Enoch *sleeper*
Pass	12.10am Euston-Glasgow *sleeper*
3.50am	3.20am Chester-Manchester Exch
6.0am	6.0am stopper to Carlisle
7.20am	11.52pm Euston-Heysham
8.15am	8.15am to Liverpool Lime Street
8.19am	7.38am Chester-Manchester Exch.
9.0am	8.22am Chester-Manchester Exch.
9.5am	9.5am to St. Helens Shaw Street
9.27am	7.40 am Llandudno - Manchester Ex
9.50am	9.10am Chester-Tyldesley-Manchester Ex
10.4am	7.10am Birmingham - Inverness
10.27am	7.5am Holyhead - Manchester Exch.
10.49am	10.49 to St. Helens Shaw Street
11.56am	6.45 Euston-Windermere/Workington
12.24pm	8.10am Holyhead-Manchester Exch
Pass	9.5am Euston-Glasgow
	The Royal Scot
12.52pm	8.20am Euston-Blackpool Central
1.9pm	1.9pm to St. Helens Shaw Street
Pass	9.50am Euston-Perth
2.18pm	2.18pm to Earlestown
2.33pm	10.30am Euston-Carlisle/Barrow
2.51pm	12.10pm Bangor -Manchester Exch.
3.10pm	10.40am Euston-Blackpool Central
Pass	11.35am Euston-Workington
Pass	1.15pm Euston-Glasgow
	The Mid-Day Scot
Pass	8am Plymouth-Glasgow
5.2pm	4.15pm Chester-Manchester Exch.
5.18pm	1.15pm Euston-Blackpool Central
5.26pm	5.26pm to St. Helens Shaw Street
5.30pm	5.30pm to Wigan via Earlestown
5.58pm	3.38pm Llandudno-Manchester Exch
6.33pm	5.55pm from Chester
7.14pm	2.20pm Euston-Blackpool
Pass	3.45pm Euston-Glasgow
	The Caledonian
8.4pm	4.25pm Holyhead-Manchester Exch.
Pass	6.40pm Birmingham-Heysham
Pass FO	4.55pm Euston-Blackpool/Barrow
8.55pm	8.55pm to Liverpool Lime Street
9.8pm	4.55pm Euston-Blackpool/Barrow
Pass	6.10pm Euston-Morecambe/Heysham
	The Ulster Express
10.12pm	6.15pm Euston-Preston/Colne
10.21pm	7.45pm Llandudno-Manchester Exch.
Pass	7.10pm Euston-Inverness sleeper
	The Royal Highlander
Pass	7.20pm Euston-Perth/Oban FO
Pass	7.20pm Euston-Stranraer *sleeper*
	The Northern Irishman

Departure Time	Train
12.0am	12am to Chester
12.14am MX	6.50pm Glasgow-Euston *12.28 MO*
Pass	9.25pm Glasgow-Euston *sleeper*
Pass	10.20pm Glasgow-Euston *sleeper*
Pass	9pm Perth-Euston *sleeper*
Pass	10.25pm Glasgow-Euston *sleeper*
Pass MX	10.10pm Stranrear-Euston
	The Northern Irishman
Pass MO	5.5pm Inverness-Euston *sleeper*
Pass MX	5.40pm Inverness-Euston *sleeper*
	The Royal Highlander
Pass	11.15pm Glasgow-Birmingham *sleeper*
5.43am	5.18am from St. Helens Shaw Street
6.52am	5.30am Preston-Crewe
7.16am	6.42am from St. Helens Shaw Street
7.28am	7.28am to Chester
7.40am	7.8am from Wigan
7.56am	6.42am Lancaster-Euston
Pass MX	6.55am Heysham-Euston
8.44am	7.52am Manchester Exch - Chester.
8.58am	8.39am from Wigan
9.13am	8.35am Manchester Exch-Chester.
9.19am	7.55am Blackpool Central-Euston
9.32am	9.3am from St. Helens Shaw Street
10.53am	6.10am Carlisle-Crewe
11.7am	10.25am Manchester Exch.-Chester
11.39am	10.57am from St.Helens Shaw Street
Pass	6.30am Workington-Euston
12.7pm SX	8.40am Carlisle - Euston
12.37pm	11.55pm Manchester Exch.-Holyhead
Pass	8.30am Glasgow-Euston *The Caledonian*
1.39pm	12noon Blackpool - Crewe *(Euston FO)*
1.40pm	1.15pm from St. Helens Shaw Street
2.17pm WO	1.35pm Manchester Exch-Llandudno
Pass	10am Glasgow-Euston *The Royal Scot*
Pass	10.5am Glasgow-Plymouth
Pass	9am Perth/10.53 Workington-Euston
4.16pm	2.30pm Morecambe-Crewe *Euston FO*
5.1pm	4.30pm Manchester Exch-Llandudno
5.15pm	5.15pm to Chester
5.20pm	5.20pm to Crewe
5.43pm	5.7pm Manchester Exch. - Chester
5.55pm	5.29pm from St. Helens Shaw Street
6.2pm	5.31pm from Wigan
Pass	1.15pm Glasgow-Euston *The Mid-Day Scot*
6.16pm	5.35pm Manchester Ex. - Llandudno
Pass	12.10pm Perth-Euston
6.39pm	6.39pm to Crewe
6.55pm	5.5pm Blackpool Central-Euston
8.13pm	8.13pm to Crewe
8.18pm	7.25pm Manchester Exch.-Chester
10.3pm	9.12pm Manchester Exch-Chester
10.29pm	7.2pm from Carlisle
10.56pm	10.20pm Manchester Ex-Holyhead
11.27pm	6.28pm Workington-Euston

Above: Class 47 diesel No. D1548 sets off south from Bank Quay station and passes Warrington No. 1 signal box while working a long West Coast Main Line stopping train, reporting No. 2A45, during the transition from maroon to blue and grey coaches.

Below: With Arpley yards down below on the right and Warrington No. 1 box behind it, Britannia Pacific 70032 *Tennyson* storms away from Bank Quay with the Carlisle to Crewe vans in 1967.

Above: Crossing the bridge carrying the Warrington-Crewe section of the West Coast Main Line over the River Mersey with an Up express is Britannia No. 70049 *Solway Firth*. At one time the few named after Firths were the only Britannias to be seen at Warrington.

Below: All the power and glory of a big steam engine in full cry is captured in this remarkable picture. Britannia No. 70029 *Shooting Star* makes a volcanic assault on the climb past Walton New Junction to the Manchester Ship Canal bridge with the Carlisle to Crewe parcels on 2nd May, 1967.

Above: Another one to get the sences racing. This time it is **70033** *Charles Dickens* on a southbound express that is blasting its way up to Acton Grange.

Below: Black Five 4-6-0 No. 45140 is just as impressive, dragging its train of covered hopper wagons up the grade, away from the Mersey bridge and past Walton New Junction signal box

Above: Sterile compared with the previous pictures it may be, but the sight of a green-liveried English Electric Type 4(class 40) heading a London express across the Mersey bridge is nevertheless one to stir the emotions. The box and semaphore signals went during resignalling in the early 1970s, just before the whole West Coast main line through Warrington was electrified.

SHORT MEMORIES

22.3.65: Steam replaces DMUs on Manchester-North Wales 'Club' trains following complaints from commuters about the riding of the diesels. Class 5 45285 works the 16.30 from Manchester on 26.3.65.

Left: Hard but happy work for the signalman in Walton New Junction box. The diagramme shows the layout at this point.

Above: A traditional railway scene - the platelayer stands back as Black Five No.45072 makes solid progress past Walton New Junction box with an Up fitted freight.

Below: Rolling effortlessly towards Acton Grange canal bridge with an Up fitted freight is the last working Royal Scot, the now preserved 46115 *Scots Guardsman.*

Above: The power and majesty of the Coronation class is well evident as 46238 *City of Carlisle* passes Acton Grange Junction with northbound express 1L16 on 3rd August, 1963. TheChester line approaches from the left. *(Graham Kaye)*

Below: The scene at Acton Grange after the appalling collision between the Euston to Stranraer boat train and some runaway soda ash wagons on 13th May, 1966. Breakdown cranes are on the scene along with the emergency services, including the Auxiliary Fire Service vehicle in the right foreground.

One of the worst accidents in the Warrington area within living memory was the collision at Acton Grange on 13th May, 1966.

Late that evening the 20.40 Euston to Stranraer boat train hauled by class 40 diesel No. D322 ran into covered hopper wagons loaded with soda ash which had broken loose from a Northwich - St. Helens freight.

The Crewe driver and second man in D322's cab were both killed. The double tragedy cast a shadow over the daily routine of the railway around Warrington for a long time and is still rooted in the memories of long-serving rail staff.

In his accident report, railway inspecting officer Col. W.P. Reed concluded that the root cause of the crash was a loose screw coupling between the second and third wagons. The coupling had lifted from the drawhook, possibly during a snatch, and the wagons had broken loose, the guard's hand brake being insufficient to stop them running back down the gradient.

Above: Train No. 1N82, descending the steep incline from Acton Grange to Walton Old Junction, is heading for the North Eastern Region. Black Five 4-6-0 No. 44946 of Mirfield shed will take the trainload of holidaymakers returning from North Wales back to the West Riding via Arpley Junction, Stockport and Stalybridge.

Below: Also coming down the bank, WD 2-8-0 No. 90281 with a Wirral DC lines electric multiple unit en-route from Birkenhead to Horwich works.

Above: A general view of Walton Old Junction yard looking south with Black Five No. 45039 and WD 2-8-0 90397. On the right, the Crewe line climbs the embankment to the ship canal bridge.

Below: A pleasing portrait of the unique Black Five with Stephenson's link motion instead of the more common Walschaerts valve gear. No. 44767, stood in Walton Old Junction yard, was still hauling special trains on the main line in 1996.

SHORT MEMORIES

Above: With the Laporte chemical works on its left, 9F 2-10-0 No. 92131 makes a formidable sight as it rolls down to Walton Old Junction with an oil train from the Shell refineries at Stanlow.

Below: Walton Old Junction yard staff and train crew pose with class 3F 0-6-0T No. 47395 during a break in shunting operations. The bridge carrying the West Coast main line over the River Mersey looms above their heads.

9.3.65: The Transport Minister approves withdrawal of the Bank Quay-St. Helens local service and closure of Vulcan Halt.

13.3.65: Dallam shed receives a big influx of 9Fs - Nos. 92048/9/53/5/8/9/70/8/86/116/9/24/6/56/60/3. They arrive after being displaced by diesels from Midland line depots at Leicester, Kettering and Toton.

5.5.65: Class 40 No. D371 hauls the Freightliner test train 3Z70 including dynamometer car through Warrington.

Above: 8F 2-8-0 No. 48722 runs round its Dallam to Godley Junction empty wagon train on the old Chester line which was, and still is, regularly used for this purpose. The roller coaster incline of the new Chester line to the ship canal bridge is visible through the mist above the 8F's tender. *(Trevor Rowe)*

Below: Black Five 4-6-0 No. 45092 gets moving from Walton Old Junction yard with a short mixed express goods. The headlamps show that vacuum brake was operative over at least 20 per cent of the train. In 1996 this yard was used mainly for stabling coal wagons.

Decorated Crabs at Walton Old Junction.
Above: Hughes-Fowler 2-6-0 No. 42727 of Birkenhead, with white front end trimmings, trundles a long Through Freight down from Acton Grange in 1966.

Below: Another with white trimmings, 42942, heads a similar class of freight in the other direction. The train has a banking engine, as was often the case for the slog up to the canal bridge.

In the 1960s Trevor Rowe worked as a goods guard at Warrington, a signalbox lad at Dallam Branch Sidings, and a signalman at Walton Old Junction.

His guard's training was at Warrington Central goods offices where there was a depot for goods guards.

He recalls: "The first thing I remember about Central early on a morning was seeing a 4F boiling up behind the station. There was no engine shed there, but two roads along the town side of the station for stabling.

"It was a big goods yard with a three-storey warehouse. Towards the east end, the yard narrowed over Battersby Lane and then widened out again into a double-ended group of sidings.

"The last signalbox going east out of Central was called Workshops. It was a little rickety building named after the signal and telegraph workshops for the whole Cheshire Lines which were once there and which, I believe, were eventually swallowed up by Rylands' wire works.

"We had quite a few trip workings to do around Warrington. One of them, Target 75, did 25 miles each way just to get a mile across town from Arpley sidings to Central Goods and back. It had to run via Skelton Junction and Glazebrook. There was a connection up to the CLC at Froghall but it went through the English Steel Company's works so could not be used for through traffic. A wagon once ran away down this line from the CLC, rolling all the way to Dallam Sidings."

Trevor Rowe's moment of glory came when he derailed a 9F 2-10-0 during his spell as signalman at Walton Old Junction.

He explains: "There was a legitimate move which involved sending engines 'wrong road' to reach one of four shunting necks at Arpley sidings, passing a shunt signal at danger on the way to Twelve Arches bridge. The road was protected against such wrong line movements by a set of trap points but we could reset them once the move had been accepted by Arpley Junction box.

On this particular day, I was shouting to the fireman of 92160, which was due to pick up a goods to Gowhole yard, Derbyshire, that the Arpley shunters wanted them on No.3 neck when Arpley Junction box accepted the loco on the bell code. I told him he could go but

clean forgot about resetting the traps and 92160 went off the road."

Another 'wrong road' movement involved shunt engines working at Froghall sidings.

"There were about 15 sidings at Froghall plus those serving Whitecross wire works and sometimes the pilot needed to come to Dallam shed for water. They would return to Froghall 'wrong road' along the Down Slow. It was a move allowed from Dallam to Bank Quay as shown on the block card in Dallam Branch Sidings box - the block card listed the movements you could undertake contrary to the normal Absolute Block signalling.

"The Down Slow at Dallam was signalled by Permissive Block but we could use it for passenger trains by fixing a plate on the block instruments to remind us that we had a passenger train on. We also had to come to a clear understanding with the next box that we had a passenger train on the line.

"Dallam was not the most celubrious place to eat your lunch. You always had a smell to go with it whichever way the wind blew, what with the gas works, the steel works, a brewery, Longford's wire works, a scrap yard and the Shed. Blue, oily smoke came out of black holes in the wall of Longford's and with it an awful stench.

"Traffic at Dallam yard included grain for Walker's brewery and wagons of steaming spent hops coming out. They were always covered in sparrows looking for seeds.

"Also at Dallam was Fullerlove's wagon repair yard which repaired coal wagons, and down the branch, beyond the level crossing, the Co-op coal yard.

"At Walton Old Junction, where there was always a smell of cardboard from the Thames Board mills, we had a local arrangement which allowed rakes of wagons to be worked from Winwick Quay or Dallam without a brake van at the rear. This was so they were ready for reversing to Arpley Junction and the Low Level line.

"Instead of a brake van we put a tail lamp on the last wagon, or if there was no lamp available we used anything to hand, even an old bucket would do so long as everyone understood the tail lamp was a bucket.

"We moved up to 40 Dallam to Godley Junction empties like this and they could go through four or five block sections on the way."

Above: The Wigan Springs Branch breakdown crane busy rerailing 9F No. 92160 which Trevor Rowe managed to derail during his first month at Walton Old Junction box. Arthur Chester gleefully presented him with this picture a few days later.

Left: The youthful Trevor Rowe(left) inside Walton Old Junction box with fellow signalman Eddie Owen during October, 1965. All the old mechanical boxes on the West Coast main line through Warrington, including this one, were swept away by resignalling in 1972.

Above: A foreigner in the camp - at least so far as the LNW section is concerned. The 1M48 reporting number chalked on the smokebox door confirms that B1 4-6-0 No. 61313 of Canklow(Rotherham) shed is heading a train from the Eastern Region. Passing Walton Old Junction in the direction of Chester and North Wales, it has probably come from Sheffield.

Below: Another express to North Wales, this time from Manchester with more familiar motive power. Patricroft-based BR class 5 No. 73157 passes one of Dallam's two BR/Gardener 204hp(class 03) diesel shunters in Walton Old Junction yard while heading what may well be the 4.30pm Manchester Exchange to Llandudno 'Club' train in 1963 or 64.

Above: Jubilee 4-6-0 No. 45647 *Sturdee* of Farnley Junction, Leeds, is almost certainly heading a summer Saturday Leeds to Llandudno express which has reached Walton Old Junction via Stalybridge, Stockport and Arpley Junction. It should not find the climb to Acton Grange too difficult, not with a 9F as banker.

Below: Stoke-based 8F No. 48353 digs in with a southbound express goods, passing Walton Old Junction box on one side and Shrewsbury Black Five 44963 on the other.

When Great Western men from the Chester or Wrexham areas worked to Walton Old Junction they always insisted on turning their brake van on a turntable.

They had single ended vans and there was no way they would work back with the open end facing inwards - it always had to face out from the back of the train.

Above: Britannia No. 70034 *Thomas Hardy* makes a dramatic exit past Walton Old Junction.

Below: A long train of mineral wagons headed by Croes Nwydd(Wrexham) Black Five No. 45130 receives the assistance of a banker while passing classmate 45138 on its way up to Acton Grange. On the left is the entrance to Walton Old Junction yard.

Above: Class 9F 2-10-0 No. 92126 erupts into action while heading a freight past Walton Old Junction box and up to Acton Grange in November, 1964. The huge expanse of the Thames Board mills fills the distant background.

The 1977 LM Region Sectional Appendix listed the former Warrington & Stockport line between Arpley Junction and Walton Old Junction as being just under a mile long, signalled as a passenger line(Absolute Block) with Permissive Block for freight trains, and with a maximum speed of 45 mph.

Below: On the north side of the Mersey, at the south end of Arpley sidings. Stanier Black Five 4-6-0 No. 45067 prepares an express freight consisting of a variety of vans as classmate 44809 waits for the road on the Arpley Junction-Walton Old Junction line.

Above: Happily, Arpley sidings, situated just south of Bank Quay station, below the east side of the main line, were still a busy freight hub in 1996. This was how they looked more than 30 yars before when even busier. On the right is the 15-road 'old' side of the yard, then the Walton Old Junction-Arpley Junction line. The 350hp diesel on the left is shunting the later nine-road extension while a 4F is on the line which descends steeply from Bank Quay. The Black Five and water tank are on the Down Through Siding, alias 'The Hole' which went under the main line to the Down side at Bank Quay as well as Crosfield's High Sidings and the transporter bridge which took wagons across the Mersey to part of Crosfield's works.

Below: 4F 0-6-0 No. 44349 comes under the West Coast Main Line and emerges from 'The Hole' into Arpley yard with a working known as 'N' Trip

SHORT MEMORIES

Above: Yard staff stop and watch as 9F No. 92102 gets on its way from the old side of the yard at Arpley with special express freight No. 4Z17. No less than four other engines - two 350hp shunters, 4F No. 44522 and a Black Five - plus a wide range of wagons - occupy this part of the yard.

5.2.66: Class 20 diesel D8128 is allocated to Dallam but moves on to Tinsley, Eastern Region, after just two weeks.

18.4.66: The remaining Manchester Central-Warrington Central steam workings give way to DMUs

May, 1966: Standard class 5 4-6-0s, some with Caprotti valve gear, start working Manchester-North Wales 'Club' trains following transfer of duties from Llandudno Junction shed to Patricroft.

2.7.66: 45581 *Bihar & Orissa* is on a Sats Only Leeds-Lladudno.

Below: A close-up of 44522 on trip duty and complete with smokebox adornment and yellow cab stripe forbidding it to work on electrified lines south of Crewe. Beyond the engine are the Thames Board mills and St. James church, Latchford.

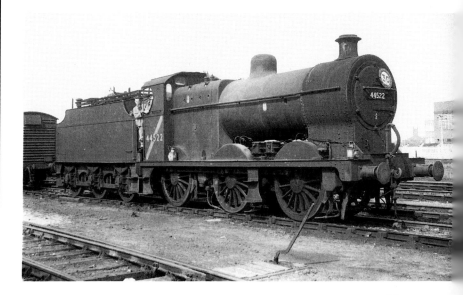

Above: An 8F 2-8-0 plods round the curve from Arpley Junction and under Slutchers Lane bridge with a string of empty coal wagons. Enginemen going the other way had plenty of time to make use of the water tank while waiting at the tall signal. Such were the long delays at this spot awaiting paths on to the Low Level line, that crews called it the 'Golden Mile' because of the overtime they could earn.

SHORT MEMORIES

28.5.66: BR 5MT 4-6-0 73006 passes Bank Quay with a Whit Monday 8.5am Manchester Exchange to Caernarvon relief. Britannia 70012 *John of Gaunt* is on a Holyhead-Manchester relief.

March 1967: Newly restored A4 Pacific No. 4498 *Sir Nigel Gresley* works through Warrington with an evening Crewe-Preston parcels and the 5.35am Preston-Crewe semi-fast for several days while running-in from Crewe works.

22.7.67: Sulzer Type 2 diesel D5273 allocated to Dallam for crew training.

Below: With the Thames Board mills on the right, 8F No. 48324 is passing the south end of Arpley sidings with a mixed goods. The main line from Bank Quay to Walton Old Junction, often used by Chester trains, comes down on the left.

Above: This wonderful picture brings back memories of the days when 2-6-2Ts shuffled along with local passenger trains to and from Bank Quay's low level platforms. Sutton Oak-based Ivatt class 2 No. 41286 takes water at Arpley Junction on 28th February, 1966 before taking its Locomotive Club of Great Britain push-pull railtour off to Altrincham. Arpley goods shed is on the right and Slutcher's Lane bridge in the background, while Sutton Oak guard J. Arthur Davies watches over the watering process.

ALONG THE LOW LEVEL LINE

Below: Arpley Junction viewed from Slutchers Lane bridge more than 15 years after the above picture above was taken.
Aprley Junction signal box is on the left, the site of the station and engine shed in the centre background and the huge Garton's seed warehouse on the right. This was still a busy spot in late 1996 with plenty of class 31, 37, 56 and 60 diesels using the stabling sidings and coal trains reversing on their way to and from Fiddler's Ferry power station, although Garton's warehouse and the pre-fab offices have gone along with the class 20, 25 and 40 locos. The smaller building to the left of Garton's warehouse is offices and in 1996 is still used by railway signal engineers.
(Malcolm Roughley)

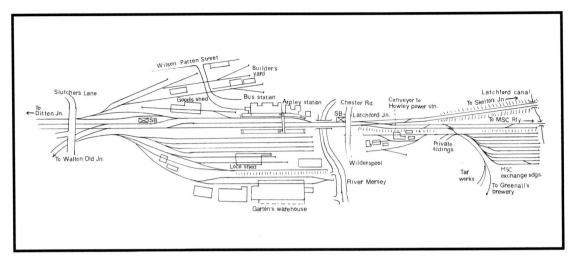

Above: The layout at Arpley as it was in 1963. *(Not to scale)*

Above: The two-road engine shed at Arpley was a sub-shed of Dallam so the engines which worked from it carried the 8B shed code. Arpley shed closed on 27th May, 1963 following withdrawal of the Low Level line passenger service the previous year and dieselisation of other local services. It was subsequently demolished but the site probably sees more locomotives stabled there in 1996 than in April, 1959 when this picture of Stanier class 3 2-6-2T No. 40201 was taken. *(Peter Hughes/Colour-Rail)*

In 1957 Arpley station and goods depot were equipped to deal with livestock but not horse boxes, motor vehicles, furniture vans, portable engines or machines on wheels. The goods depot had a crane of 10 ton maximum capacity.

In 1961, the Warrington district goods manager's offices were at Arpley. The goods manager then was a Mr. W. H. Hardy.

In 1977 the Low Level line was classed as a goods line with Absolute Block signalling and a maximum speed of 40mph.

Warrington area signal boxes were at Latchford(9miles 61chains), Arpley Jn.(11m 2ch), Crosfield's Crossing(11m 35ch), Litton's Mill level crossing(11m 45ch), and Monk's Siding(11m 70ch).

The 1972 resignalling did not extend to the Low Level line and all these manual boxes, except Latchford, were still in use in 1996.

The LCGB railtour hauled by 41286 leaves Arpley and crosses Wilderspool bridge over the River Mersey. The signal was exceptionally tall so that it could be seen from the bend approaching Arpley Junction on the line from Walton Old Junction

PASSENGER TRAINS FROM BANK QUAY LOW LEVEL 2.11.59 - 12.6.60

TIME	TRAIN
6.25am SX	6.25 to Warwick Road
6.52am	6.14 Runcorn-Timperley
8.5am	7.34 Runcorn-Warwick Road
8.35am	7.57 Runcorn-Manchester Oxford Rd
8.54am SX	7.58 from Liverpool Lime St.
8.57am SO	8.3 from Liverpool Lime St.
12.52-1.4pm SO	12.5 Liverpool Lime Street-Manchester Oxford Rd.
4.18pm SX	4.18 to Warwick Road
4.18pm SO	4.18 to Manchester Oxford Rd
5.29-37pm SX	4.43 Liverpool Lime St-Manchester Oxford Rd
6.52pm SX	6pm from Liverpool Lime St.
7.19pm SO	6.30 from Liverpool Lime St.
9pm SO	9pm to Manchester Oxford Rd
11.15pm-midnight	10.35pm Liverpool Lime Street-Stockport Edgeley
	Through carriages to Leeds and York

TIME	TRAIN
7.28am SX	7.28 to Runcorn
7.28am SO	7.28 to Ditton Jn.
8.20am SX	7.55 from Broadheath
8.20am SO	7.40 from Timperley
8.37-42am SX	7.50 Warwick Rd-Ditton Jn
1.11-31pm SO	12.25pm Manchester Oxford Rd-Runcorn
5.5-13pm	4.7pm Manchester Oxford Rd-Liverpool Lime Street
5.44pm SX	5.3 from Warwick Rd
5.46pm SO	5.6 from Warwick Rd
6.13pm SO	5.27 from Manchester Oxford Rd
6.18pm SX	5.34 from Stretford
7.52pm SX	7pm from Manchester Oxford Rd
8.7pm SO	7.20 from Warwick Rd
11.29pm SO	10.43 from Manchester Oxford Rd

Going west, trains called at Widnes South, and Runcorn or Ditton Jn. Going east they called at Latchford, Lymm, Heatley & Warburton, Dunham Massey, Broadheath, Timperley, Brooklands, Sale, Stretford, Warwick Rd., Old Trafford, Knott Mill & Deansgate and Oxford Rd. At the time, trains were suspended between Manchester Oxford Rd. and London Rd owing to electrification work and some were turning round short of Manchester.

On 6th April, 1968, the LCGB ran a tour over the Low Level line hauled by now preserved Black Five 4-6-0 No. 45305. Top: No. 45305 climbing away from Warrington and up past Latchford signal box to the canal bridge. *(Trevor Rowe)*

Centre: The going away view shows 45305 passing the site of Latchford 'new' station and the abandoned goods yard with the bridge ahead.
The station site became a garden centre but the main line track remained, closed to through traffic. *(Trevor Rowe)*

Bottom: This view at Latchford shows just how tall the ship canal bridges had to be. The disused bridge still stood in 1996 but was rumoured for early demolition. *(Stephen Chapman)*

EXCHANGE OF TRAFFIC BETWEEN BR AND MANCHESTER SHIP CANAL COMPANY: MSC locomotives are allowed to work over the Latchford Old lines between the canal bridge and the entrance to Greenall's siding. Wagons must be drawn by the MSC locomotives and detached in the siding furthest from the main line.

MSC locomotives must not go over the canal bridge until it has been ascertained that the line is clear and that no BR locomotive is working in either of the sidings between the canal bridge and the entrance to Greenall's siding. If a BR locomotive is working in the sidings, the permission of the Guard or Shunter in charge of it must be obtained before the MSC train proceeds on to the Latchford Old lines.

If a BR locomotive is working in the sidings beyond the entrance to Greenall's sidings, the MSC locomotive must not foul the crossing between the sidings and Greenall's siding without obtaining permission from the BR Guard or Shunter.

Before making any movement which will foul the third line, BR Guards and Shunters must place to danger the signal controlling movements from that line...*LMR Sectional Appendix 1977*

The winter 1959/60 working timetable listed 56 booked freight trains per 24 hours past Arpley Junction in the Up(eastbound) direction on Tuesdays to Fridays and 37 in the Down(westbound) direction. Other trains ran on certain days, some just one day a week.

Many trains were at night when one would pass through Arpley Junction in one direction or other on average every 10 minutes. Often two or more trains were there at a time, many stopping for water, to change crews or let other trains pass. Certain Up trains stopped instead at Bank Quay.

The Down trains were mostly going to Widnes West Deviation Junction, Ravenhead Sidings, Birkenhead, Edge Hill, Mold Junction, were taking coal and coke from Yorkshire and the East Midlands to Garston dock, or were returning empty tanks to the Stanlow refineries.

In the Up direction, oil trains ran from Stanlow to Penistone, Stow Park, Morton and York, while empty coal and coke wagons returned to Kirkby Sidings, Crofton Hall, Gowhole and Cheadle Junction. Trains also ran from Mold Junction to Dewsnap, and Widnes Marsh's Sidings, Birkenhead, Garston and Edge Hill to Healey Mills.

Notable workings included the forerunners of today's automotive services, 4E90 and 4E91, the 1.52pm and 3.10pm Ford's Sidings to Immingham and the 4M40 and 4M41 return, and there were 10 class 4 paths to run as required from Garston to Healey Mills, Manchester, Dewsnap, Cheadle Sidings and Rotherham - likely as not they were banana trains to run when the banana boats docked.

Local trips included 9T75 8.40am and 3.10pm Arpley-Monk's Sidings, and 9T85 8.30am Arpley-Latchford and 9.20am return.

Numerous light engines ran, especially westbound in the afternoon from sheds further east, mainly Heaton Mersey, to work evening freights from Garston.

On the Low Level line west of Bank Quay, a part of Warrington's railway rarely seen or photographed by enhusiasts.
In 1996, little had changed since this late 1980s view of a class 08 350hp diesel shunter approaching Monk's Siding signal box on its way to Garston.
The connections to the steelworks, closed in spring, 1986, had already been removed.
(Malcom Roughley)

Three manual signal boxes still in use on the Low Level line.

Top: Monk's Siding box with its hipped roof sees less action since the steelworks closed but in 1996 it still dealt with a procession of coal trains to Fiddler's Ferry power station.

Centre: Less than half a mile towards Warrington, is Litton's Mill signal box and level crossing.
The box marks the site of the St. Helens Canal and Railway Company's temporary White Cross station.

Bottom: Crosfield's Crossing, as its name implies, is in the midst of the vast Lever Brothers soap works and controls the crossing linking two parts of the plant.
Built in 1913, Crosfield's is an LNWR Type 4 box fitted with an 18 lever tumbler frame controlling a section under a mile long.
(All Stephen Chapman)

Up freight trains requiring to work Crosfield's siding must stop at Litton's Mill and the guard advise the signalman how many wagons are on the train. Trains not more than 11 single wagon lengths may go straight to the siding, guards taking care to leave trains clear of the crossing.
Longer trains must be left to the rear of the crossing, the engine and front portion proceeding to the siding to do its work, returning for the rest of the train afterwards. *LMR Sectional Apendix, 1977.*

Above: Warrington Central station on New Year's day, 1974, looking towards Liverpool and with a class 108 Derby Works DMU about to leave with a local service to Manchester. *(Gordon Coltas)*

THE CHESHIRE LINES COMMITTEE

Below: Central's famous Cheshire Lines goods depot on 25th May, 1975 when still in use. The yard contains an interesting assortment of freight, including one of the fast disappearing small containers, a road vehicle on a wagon and, behind 350hp diesel shunter No. 08670, a loading ramp for cars. *(Gordon Coltas)*

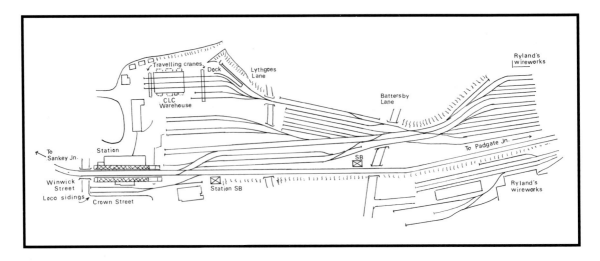

Above: Warrington Central in 1963. *(Not to scale)*

Left: Change at Central in 1971. The standard London Midland Region box still operational in 1996 has just been built and will replace the Manchester, Sheffield and Lincolnshire Railway-style Warrington Station box beyond it. Also, the semaphore signals will be replaced by colour lights. A class 108 Derby Works DMU is just emerging from the sidings. *(P. Norton collection)*

The 1957 BTC Handbook of Stations listed Warrington Central as able to deal with furniture vans, carriages, motor cars, portable engines and machines on wheels, livestock, horse boxes and prize cattle vans, by passenger or parcels train, though much of the traffic was steel. The goods depot had a crane with a maximum lift of 7.5 tons plus mobile cranes.

Central Goods closed in February, 1983 when facilities were transferred to a new BR terminal at Dallam Branch Sidings. Facilities there from 1983 were handling staff, a Jones 10/15 ton crane and a 10 ton freight lifter. A second, privately-run, freight terminal was opened on the adjacent site of Dallam Forge steelworks in 1986.

Top: The grand Warrington Central station frontage as it was in May, 1975.

Centre: Central station from Winwick Street on the same day showing how obscure the main entrance was.
A new entrance complete with ticket office, booking hall and newsagents was opened in place of the big wall with posters on it in 1983.
The bridge on the right, still with 'Central Station' on it then, dated from reconstrution in 1934.
(Both Gordon Coltas)

Bottom: Central station looking towards Liverpool before the original canopies were replaced by the flat roof variety.
(Lens of Sutton)

"Until the early 1950s the Great Central Director 4-4-0s worked passenger trains to Central and then it all changed to a whole variety of ex-LMS tanks - Stanier 2-6-2Ts, Fairburn and Stanier 2-6-4Ts. There was an intense passenger service and at teatime the platforms were very crowded, a train coming about every 12 minutes. In 1960 it became the first line in this part of the country to have DMUs but there was still a lot of steam. My morning train to journalist's college in Manchester in 1961/62 was always a Black Five.
"There was a buffet on the Manchester platform and J10 0-6-0s shunted in the sidings, I will always remember their flowerpot chimneys" - *Peter Kelly.*

On Mondays to Fridays between 2nd November, 1959 and 12th June, 1960 54 trains left Warrington Central in the eastbound direction and 60 in the westbound direction.

Hourly expresses between Manchester Central and Liverpool Central generally left Warrington in both directions at 56 minutes past the hour.

Local trains followed less of a regular pattern but were more frequent between Warrington and Liverpool with 25 to Liverpool and 15 to Manchester plus corresponding services the other way and extra trains in the morning and evening rush hours.

Other services were Stockport Tivoit Dale trains which left Warrington at 5.49am(a service from Liverpool), 12.35pm, 5.15pm and 5.42pm(another from Liverpool). Trains arrived from Stockport at 6.14am, 8.2am(to Liverpool), and 4.4pm. The Stockport trains joined and left the Warrington-Manchester line at Glazebrook.

Aintree-Manchester trains called at Warrington Central at 7.28am, 8.29am and 8.36am, the latter terminating at Warrington.

One Manchester-Aintree train called at 5.35pm and one Aintree train started from Warrington at 6pm.

The 9.30am Liverpool-Manchester express ran through to Hull and the 2.30pm to Nottingham Midland. The 11.30am Manchester to Liverpool conveyed a through carriage from Nottingham and the 8pm from Manchester a through carriage from Hull.

Warrington Central had its own London service - an overnight train. The 9.30pm Liverpool Central to London Marylebone left at 9.57 and the 10pm from Marylebone, which did not run on Sunday nights/Monday mornings, arrived at 5.10am.

Two other expresses each way ran non-stop via the avoiding line. They were the 1.15pm Liverpool Central to Harwich boat train, and the 4.52pm Liverpool Central to Hull which ran non-stop to Manchester in 42 minutes, the 8am Harwich to Liverpool, passing around 2.40pm, and the 10.8am from Manchester which ran non-stop to Liverpool in just 38 minutes.

In 1996 Central was served by 51 express and local train to Manchester and 56 to Liverpool.

The J10 0-6-0s, built by the Manchester, Sheffield and Lincolnshire Railway from 1892 to the design of T. Parker, were a regular feature of the CLC. LNER No. 5125 was already near the end of its life in this moody late 1940s scene. *(Gordon Coltas)*

Right: Two and a half miles west of Warrington Central is Sankey for Penketh station.
The architectural style of this and other CLC stations is pure MSLR and virtually identical to that company's own stations on the other side of the Pennines.
This was Sankey for Penketh looking east, still with BR totem name boards in place, in May, 1975.
(Gordon Coltas)

In winter 1959/60 the Warrington Central-Manchester Central second class return fare was three shillings and ninepenc(about 19p). In 1961 the Bank Quay-Euston second class return fare was 77 shillings(£3.85).

In 1977 the CLC had a maximum line speed of 75mph with the curving loop through Central station restricted to 50mph. The Down and Up Goods loops at Central were 20mph.
Signalling between Glazebrook and Allerton Jn. was Absolute Block with Track Circuit Block east of Glazebrook.

Above: Even this enamel sign, still proclaiming the station's identity in May, 1996, is becoming a railway memory. Not only was British Rail on the verge of disappearing in the wake of privatisation but the white lettering on 'rail blue' background, is a survivor from the late 1960s when the BR corporate identity replaced the regional colour schemes. *(Stephen Chapman).*

Right: British Rail will eventually be as much a part of history as the Cheshire Lines Committee, recalled on this weight restriction notice still on the overbridge at Sankey in 1973. *(Gordon Coltas)*

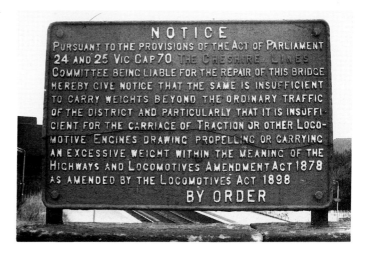

NOTICE
PURSUANT TO THE PROVISIONS OF THE ACT OF PARLIAMENT 24 AND 25 VIC CAP 70 THE CHESHIRE LINES COMMITTEE BEING LIABLE FOR THE REPAIR OF THIS BRIDGE HEREBY GIVE NOTICE THAT THE SAME IS INSUFFICIENT TO CARRY WEIGHTS BEYOND THE ORDINARY TRAFFIC OF THE DISTRICT AND PARTICULARLY THAT IT IS INSUFFICIENT FOR THE CARRIAGE OF TRACTION OR OTHER LOCOMOTIVE ENGINES DRAWING PROPELLING OR CARRYING AN EXCESSIVE WEIGHT WITHIN THE MEANING OF THE HIGHWAYS AND LOCOMOTIVES AMENDMENT ACT 1878 AS AMENDED BY THE LOCOMOTIVES ACT 1898
BY ORDER

Above: Picturesque Padgate station haunts the memories of those who remember with fondness the days of National Service in the Royal Air Force for this was where they were sent to do their basic training, the camp being alongside Padgate Junction.

The station, seen here in May, 1996, has changed little since those days except that there were staff about then. Happily, the attractive MSLR - style station buildings survive at most CLC stations.
(Stephen Chapman)

Below: A memory of the CLC avoiding line. Dallam 8F 2-8-0 No. 48033 heads an eastbound LCGB special from Sankey Junction to Padgate Junction on 23rd June, 1968, the year of the line's closure.
(Trevor Rowe)

SHORT MEMORIES

2.10.67: Dallam shed closes. D5273 is transferred to Wigan. Most steam locos, including the 9Fs, withdrawn except for 92055 which goes to Speke Junction and 92132 which is sent to Carlisle.

26.7.69: Preserved GW 4-6-0 *Clun Castle*, Black Five 5428 and Jubilee 5593 *Kolhapur* are towed in light steam via Arpley, Skelton Jn., Glazebrook and Warrington Central en-route from Tyseley to Allerton.

27.3.71: 20 special trains run over the CLC for the FA Cup semi-final between Everton and Liverpool at Old Trafford.